The Mindful Fertility Project Press
PO Box 2
Qualicum Beach, BC V9K 1S7

www.mindfulfertilityproject.com

Ordering Information:
Quantity Sales: special discounts are available on quantity purchases by fertility clinics, psychotherapy clinics, medical clinics, associations and others. For details, contact the publisher at the address above or email us at:

conceive@mindfulfertilityproject.com

Disclaimer
This book provides general information on various self relaxation exercises and images that tend to evoke feelings of peacefulness in individuals. However, it should not be relied upon as recommending or promoting any specific diagnosis or method of treatment for a particular condition, and it is not intended as a substitute for medical advice or for direct diagnosis and treatment of a medical condition by a qualified physician. Readers who have questions about a particular condition, possible treatments for that condition, or possible reactions from the condition or its treatment should consult a physician or other qualified health care professional.

The purchase of *Coloring Conception* comes with a **FREE WORKBOOK**.

Go here: www.mindfulfertilityproject.com/progress

Your workbook will help you track your cycle, your symptoms and your progress in real time.

Cover art and interior art by Arla Patch, BFA, Ed, MFA
Cover Design by Swag Design Factory
Text by Buffy Trupp, MA, RCC, LMFT

THE MINDFUL FERTILITY PROJECT

PRESENTS

Coloring Conception

STRESS REDUCTION FOR FERTILITY SUCCESS

Buffy Trupp, MA, RCC, LMFT
Illustrated by Arla Patch, BA, Ed, MFA

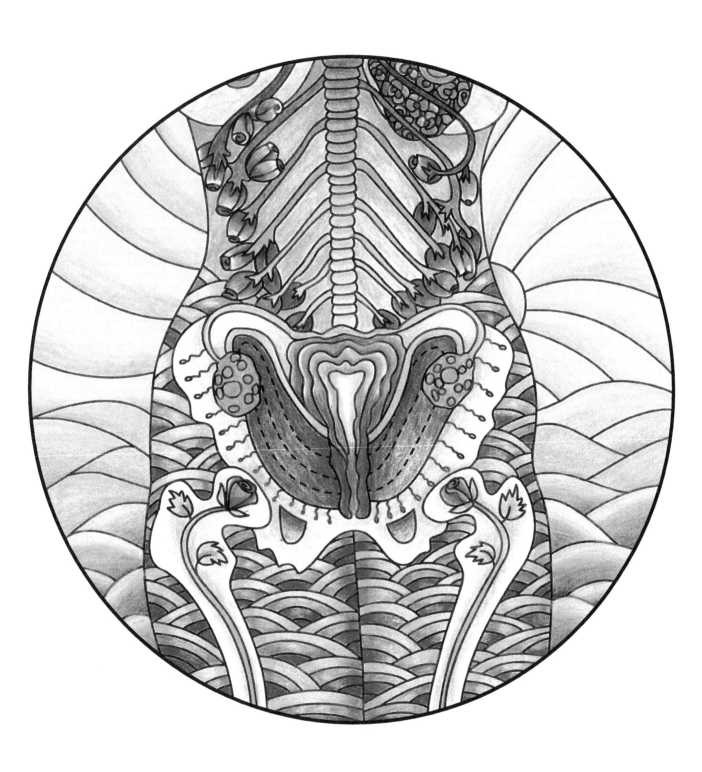

INTRODUCTION

by Buffy Trupp

Images can be very powerful fertility tools. Images, like experiences, literally shape the structure of the brain. The structure and function of the brain govern the complex task of reproduction. While trying to conceive, our brain often functions from a brain structure that was formed long ago.

Coloring Conception uses images to consciously create new neural pathways in the brain that nurture vulnerability, support the nervous system and physiologically benefit conception. The right image at the right time can open us to the present moment and direct us to the exact place inside where our life force is trying to break through. Deep within our embodied vulnerability; inside fear, shame and disappointment, is our connection to aliveness.

The truth is that a fertile life involves great attention to detail. Mindful attention in the form of coloring and self relaxation is a loving way to connect with the body while trying to conceive. The reward for embodied attention is always healing. It may begin as the healing of a particular pain - the shattered dream or the pregnant void. But what is healed, finally, is the pain that underlies all pain: the pain of aloneness, the pain of separation. Embodiment is the opposite of separation. Paying mindful attention to the body is always an act of connection.

This book is an invitation to pay attention to your body moment to moment. Let these meditations and these images guide you deep inside your body, your reproductive system and your heart. RIGHT NOW is the only moment that exists. RIGHT NOW is the only moment healing takes place. When you connect consciously with what is happening within you in each moment, however painful, and without judgment - you more simply open to life.

INTRODUCTION

by Arla Patch

Coloring is an opportunity to bring the line drawing to life. When you color, you immediately form a connection between the image and your body.

In fact science supports the powerful effect of coloring. As soon as we begin to choose a color and start looking at the shapes, our awareness shifts into the right hemisphere of our brains – the visual, spatial, perceptive, intuitive and emotional side. Our brain then produces calming alpha waves, our blood pressure goes down, our body releases endorphins and we experience a sense of well-being.

Relaxing and de-stressing in our right hemisphere we loose a sense of time, logic, sequence and are open to the free flowing reverie of our unconscious. Again, slowing down, unwinding and detangling from our busy lives. Our culture has evolved to a very left brained framework. So much is geared to and measured by left brained words and numbers – IQ scores, SAT's, hormone levels, ovarian reserve, and most of our educational and reproductive programing. It is a rare and wonderful thing indeed when we get to experience an embodied sensation and right brained consciousness and also produce a thing of beauty.

Additionally, even though the drawings might be the same for anyone who buys this book, there are an infinite number of interpretations that can create highly unique results.

The beauty in a coloring book about shifting consciousness and conceiving a child, is that there is tremendous power for transformation in the visual world. As human beings on this planet we were wired to respond to visual stimuli even before we had language. Our ability to read visual cues is what kept us alive. As an artist who uses art as a tool for healing, I have seen time and again personal transformation take place through creativity and visual art.

HOW TO USE THIS BOOK

Each day of your menstrual cycle, spend at least 20 minutes coloring and practicing the self relaxation exercises.

The first day of your period is Day 1 of your cycle. Every single woman has a different cycle length. The 28 day cycle is simply a guideline. Knowing that, it is fine to skip days, and/or repeat days. Exact accuracy is not as important as consistency.

You do not have to complete each image in one day. Of course, you may. Or, come back again and again to the images over multiple cycles if you would like. You may begin wherever you are in your cycle currently.

If you need help tracking your cycle, *Coloring Conception* comes with a free workbook.
Go here: www.mindfulfertilityproject.com/progress - your workbook will help you track your cycle, your symptoms and your progress in real time.

While coloring, slowly and silently repeat the mindful phrases to yourself. Repeat each phrase two to four times, pausing a few seconds between each repetition. When you silently and slowly repeat the phrases to yourself with a relaxed, receptive mind your peripheral circulation increases including increased circulation to your reproductive organs and cardiac and respiratory rates and rhythms begin to slow and stabilize.

When you consistently practice self relaxation to elicit the relaxation response, you can predictably measure its benefits in the body. These include: a decrease in blood pressure, diminished respiratory rate, lower pulse rate, diminished oxygen consumption, increase in alpha brain waves (associated with relaxation), and in many cases, an improved sense of mental and physical well-being.

The relaxation response is used to treat a wide variety of symptoms that are caused or exacerbated by sympathetic nervous system arousal, including challenges conceiving and carrying to term.

Use this book intuitively and most importantly, enjoy creating!

We would LOVE to see your creations! If you would like to share your artwork, please do so at #coloringconception or email us at conceive@mindfulfertilityproject.com.

COLORING TIPS

When we were children, our goal often was "to color within the lines." Depending on our age, filling in the shapes with neat edges was the focus. The color was usually solid. As adults, and using colored pencils, (I recommend *Prismacolor Colored Pencils*), we can do so much more.

With a little practice, a shape can appear to have "light" either shining on it or coming from within it. This is possible with shading...causing the color to change from dark to light.

Shading can be done in several ways. The simplest is to use more pressure for the darker side and then gradually use less pressure for a gradation to the light side of the shape.

Or going dark, light,
back to dark, etc.

We can also use texture by making our blending pencil strokes create a pattern, like cross-hatching...literally strokes repeating in parallel in one direction and then crossing back over in the opposite direction.

Crosshatching

Additionally either in a smooth, blended way or with crosshatching we can also use different colors on top of each other in a layering and blending manner.

The value of learning to shade (practice is key) is that it can bring an entirely uplifting quality into your "coloring" creating a sense of light that can enhance any drawing.

DAY 1

I feel myself surrender to the flow of life...

As I surrender, I am beginning to feel a deep and abiding love arise within me ...

My feet, knees and hips feel heavy...

Heaviness and warmth are flowing through my feet and legs...

My uterus, shedding its endometrial layer, feels relaxed and warm....

Warmth and relaxation are flowing through my uterus ...

My hands, arms and shoulders feel heavy...

Warmth and heaviness are flowing through my hands and arms...

My neck, jaw, tongue and forehead feel relaxed and smooth...

My whole body feels quiet, heavy and comfortable...

I am comfortably relaxed...

Warmth and heaviness flow into my arms, hands and fingertips...

My breathing is slow and regular...

I am aware of my calm, regular heartbeat...

As I surrender more I am increasingly aware of a deep and abiding love within me...

My mind is becoming quieter as I focus inward...

I feel still...

Deep in my mind I experience myself as relaxed, comfortable and still...

I am alert in a quiet, inward way...

As I color, I take in energizing breaths, bringing light and energy into my uterus
as it sheds its lining preparing me for pregnancy...

As I color, I bring light and energy into every cell of my body.

DAY 2

I am beginning to become more aware of my mind and body...

As I become more aware of my mind and body, I feel increasingly relaxed ...

My feet, knees and hips feel heavy...

Heaviness and warmth are flowing through my feet and legs...

My ovaries and uterus feel warm and relaxed and connected to my heart...

Warmth and relaxation are flowing through my heart, ovaries and uterus ...

My hands, arms and shoulders feel heavy...

Warmth and heaviness are flowing through my hands and arms...

My neck, jaw, tongue and forehead feel relaxed and smooth...

My whole body feels quiet, heavy and comfortable...

I am comfortably relaxed...

Warmth and heaviness flow into my arms, hands and fingertips...

My breathing is slow and regular...

I am aware of my calm, regular heartbeat...

My mind is becoming quieter as I focus inward...

I feel still...

Deep in my mind I experience myself as relaxed, comfortable and still...

Deep in my brain I experience my hypothalamus gland relaxed and still...

I am alert in a quiet, inward way...

As I color, I take in energizing breaths, bringing light and energy into my hypothalamus

gland which is behind my eyes and between my ears...

As I color, I take in energizing breaths, bringing light and energy into my heart...

As I color, I take in energizing breaths, bringing light and energy into my ovaries

and uterus...

As I color, I feel the connection between my hypothalamus gland, my heart

and my reproductive organs.

DAY 3

My mind and body are beginning to feel more and more connected...

As the connection grows between my mind and body, I feel increasingly relaxed ...

My feet, knees and hips feel heavy...

Heaviness and warmth are flowing through my feet and legs...

My uterus, ovaries, fallopian tubes, and cervix feel relaxed and warm....

Warmth and relaxation are flowing through my uterus, ovaries, fallopian tubes

and cervix ...

My hands, arms and shoulders feel heavy...

Warmth and heaviness are flowing through my hands and arms...

My neck, jaw, tongue and forehead feel relaxed and smooth...

My whole body feels quiet, heavy and comfortable...

I am comfortably relaxed...

Warmth and heaviness flow into my arms, hands and fingertips...

My breathing is slow and regular...

I am aware of my calm, regular heartbeat...

My mind is becoming quieter as I focus inward...

I feel still...

Deep in my mind I experience myself as relaxed, comfortable and still...

I am alert in a quiet, inward way...

As I color, I take energizing breaths, bringing light and energy into

my ovaries,

into the immature follicles growing within my ovaries

and into my uterus shedding its endometrial layer preparing me for pregnancy...

As I color, I take energizing breaths, bringing light and energy

into every cell of my body.

DAY 4

I am beginning to feel calm and peaceful...

As I begin to feel calm and peaceful I am more aware of my fertile body ...

My feet, knees and hips feel heavy...

Heaviness and warmth are flowing through my feet and legs...

My uterus, shedding its endometrial layer, feels relaxed and warm....

Warmth and relaxation are flowing through my uterus ...

My hands, arms and shoulders feel heavy...

Warmth and heaviness are flowing through my hands and arms...

My neck, jaw, tongue and forehead feel relaxed and smooth...

My whole body feels quiet, heavy and comfortable...

I am comfortably relaxed...

Warmth and heaviness flow into my arms, hands and fingertips...

My breathing is slow and regular...

I am aware of my calm, regular heartbeat...

My mind is becoming quieter as I focus inward...

I feel still...

My hypothalamus and pituitary glands in the center of my brain feel relaxed and warm....

Warmth and relaxation are flowing from my hypothalamus gland to my pituitary gland ...

Deep in my mind I experience myself as relaxed, comfortable and still...

I am alert in a quiet, inward way...

As I color, I take energizing breaths, bringing light and energy into my

hypothalamus and pituitary glands,

into the communication they have with one another other,

and into the communication they have with my ovaries...

As I color, I bring light and energy into my uterus shedding its endometrial layer,

preparing my body for pregnancy.

DAY 5

I am beginning to feel myself surrender more and more to the flow of life...

As I surrender more, I feel a deep and abiding love arise within me ...

My feet, knees and hips feel heavy...

Heaviness and warmth are flowing through my feet and legs...

My uterus, shedding its endometrial layer, feels relaxed and warm....

Warmth and relaxation are flowing through my uterus ...

My hands, arms and shoulders feel heavy...

Warmth and heaviness are flowing through my hands and arms...

My neck, jaw, tongue and forehead feel relaxed and smooth...

My whole body feels quiet, heavy and comfortable...

I am comfortably relaxed...

Warmth and heaviness flow into my arms, hands and fingertips...

My breathing is slow and regular...

I am aware of my calm, regular heartbeat...

As I surrender more I am increasingly aware of a deep and abiding love within me...

My mind is becoming quieter as I focus inward...

I feel still...

Deep in my mind I experience myself as relaxed, comfortable and still...

I am alert in a quiet, inward way...

As I color, I take in energizing breaths, bringing light and energy into my uterus

as it sheds its lining preparing me for pregnancy...

As I color, I bring light and energy into every cell of my body.

DAY 6

I am beginning to feel very quiet...

I am beginning to feel increasingly relaxed...

My feet, knees and hips feel heavy...

Heaviness and warmth are flowing through my feet and legs...

My uterus and ovaries feel relaxed and warm....

Warmth and relaxation are flowing through my uterus and ovaries...

My fallopian tubes are clear and open...

Relaxation is flowing through my fallopian tubes...

As I begin to feel more relaxed, my brain sends signals to my ovaries to grow follicles for ovulation...

I am beginning to feel my ovaries respond to these signals...

My hands, arms and shoulders feel heavy...

Warmth and heaviness are flowing through my hands and arms...

My neck, jaw, tongue and forehead feel relaxed and smooth...

My whole body feels quiet, heavy and comfortable...

I am comfortably relaxed...

Warmth and heaviness flow into my arms, hands and fingertips...

My breathing is slow and regular...

I am aware of my calm, regular heartbeat...

My mind is becoming quieter as I focus inward...

I feel still...

Deep in my mind I experience myself as relaxed, comfortable and still...

I am alert in a quiet, inward way...

As I color, I take energizing breaths, bringing light and energy into my

uterus,

into the immature follicles developing in my ovaries,

into every cell of my body.

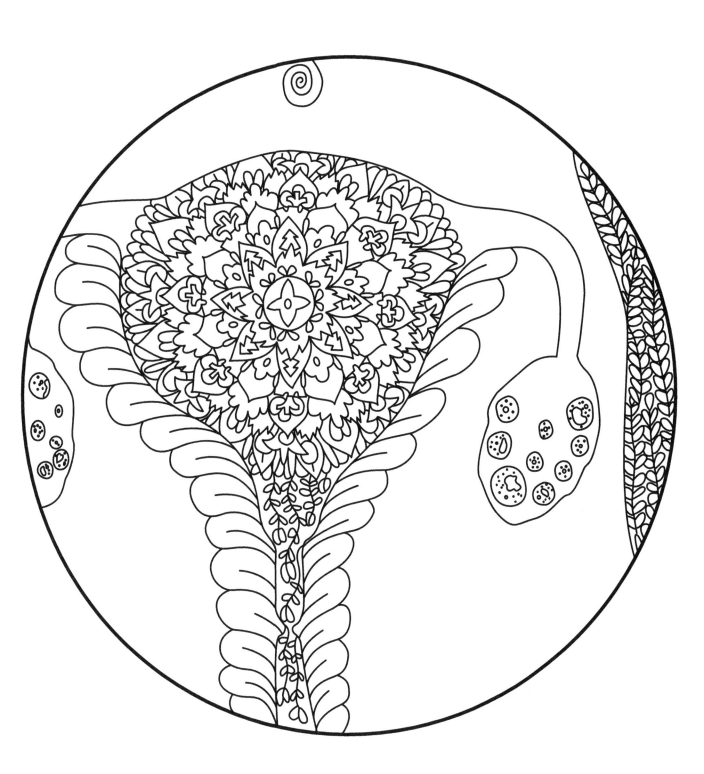

DAY 7

I am beginning to feel very quiet...

I am beginning to feel quite relaxed...

My feet, knees and hips feel heavy...

Heaviness and warmth are flowing through my feet and legs...

My uterus and ovaries feel relaxed and warm....

Warmth and relaxation are flowing through my uterus and ovaries...

As I begin to feel more at ease, my ovaries respond by developing a unique and remarkable egg(s)

within the immature follicles...

As I begin to feel more at ease, my uterus prepares to receive this special egg

later in my cycle...

My hands, arms and shoulders feel heavy...

Warmth and heaviness are flowing through my hands and arms...

My neck, jaw, tongue and forehead feel relaxed and smooth...

My whole body feels quiet, heavy and comfortable...

I am comfortably relaxed...

Warmth and heaviness flow into my arms, hands and fingertips...

My breathing is slow and regular...

I am aware of my calm, regular heartbeat...

I am aware of the feeling of deep relaxation balancing my hormones...

My mind is becoming quieter as I focus inward...

I feel still...

Deep in my mind I experience myself as relaxed, comfortable and still...

I am alert in a quiet, inward way...

As I color, I take energizing breaths, bringing light and energy into my uterus...

As I color, I bring light and energy into the immature follicles developing in my ovaries...

As I color, I bring light and energy into every cell of my body.

DAY 8

I am beginning to feel very calm...

I am beginning to feel quite relaxed...

My feet, knees and hips feel heavy...

Heaviness and warmth are flowing through my feet and legs...

My ovaries feel relaxed and warm....

Warmth and relaxation are flowing through my ovaries...

There are an abundance of healthy follicles developing in my ovaries...

My developing follicles are supported by just the right amount of follicle stimulating hormone...

My hands, arms and shoulders feel heavy...

Warmth and heaviness are flowing through my hands and arms...

My neck, jaw, tongue and forehead feel relaxed and smooth...

My whole body feels quiet, heavy and comfortable...

I am comfortably relaxed...

Warmth and heaviness flow into my arms, hands and fingertips...

My breathing is slow and regular...

I am aware of my calm, regular heartbeat...

I am aware of this deep relaxation positively influencing my hormones...

My mind is becoming quieter as I focus inward...

I feel still...

Deep in my mind I experience myself as relaxed, comfortable and still...

I am alert in a quiet, inward way...

As I color, I take energizing breaths, bringing light and energy into my ovaries

and into the immature follicles developing in my ovaries...

As I color, I bring light and energy into every cell of my body.

DAY 9

I am beginning to feel increasingly still...

I am beginning to feel profoundly relaxed...

My feet, knees and hips feel heavy...

Heaviness and warmth are flowing through my feet and legs...

My uterus feels relaxed and warm preparing to receive the egg(s)

maturing and developing in my ovary....

Warmth and relaxation are flowing through my ovaries and uterus...

My hands, arms and shoulders feel heavy...

Warmth and heaviness are flowing through my hands and arms...

Warmth and love are flowing through my heart...

My neck, jaw, tongue and forehead feel relaxed and smooth...

My whole body feels quiet, heavy and comfortable...

I am comfortably relaxed...

Warmth and heaviness flow into my arms, hands and fingertips...

My breathing is slow and regular...

I am aware of my calm, regular heartbeat...

I am aware of my deep relaxation stabilizing and balancing my hormones...

My mind is becoming quieter as I focus inward...

I feel still...

Deep in my mind I experience myself as relaxed, comfortable and still...

I am alert in a quiet, inward way...

As I color, I take energizing breaths, bringing light and energy into my

heart, my ovaries, and into my uterus...

As I color, I bring light and energy into my brain,

into my hypothalamus and pituitary glands

and then down through my heart into my reproductive organs.

DAY 10

I am beginning to feel a deep and abiding love for myself...

I am beginning to feel present for my mind and body...

My feet, knees and hips feel heavy...

Love and warmth are flowing through my feet and legs...

My uterus feels relaxed and warm preparing to receive the egg(s)

developing in my ovary....

Warmth and love are flowing through my ovaries and uterus...

My hands, arms and shoulders feel heavy...

Warmth and heaviness are flowing through my hands and arms...

Warmth and love are flowing through my heart...

My neck, jaw, tongue and forehead feel relaxed and smooth...

My whole body feels quiet, heavy and comfortable...

I am comfortably relaxed...

Warmth and heaviness flow into my arms, hands and fingertips...

My breathing is slow and regular...

I am aware of my calm, regular heartbeat...

I am aware of a deep and abiding love within me...

My mind is becoming quieter as I focus inward...

I feel still...

Deep in my mind I experience myself as relaxed, comfortable and still...

I am alert in a quiet, inward way...

As I color, I take energizing breaths, bringing love and energy into my

ovaries, into my uterus and into my heart...

As I color, I bring love and energy into my brain,

and into my hypothalamus and pituitary glands

as they communicate with my heart

and reproductive organs

preparing me for ovulation.

DAY 11

I am beginning to feel increasingly present in my mind and body...

The more present I am, the more relaxed I feel...

My feet, knees and hips feel heavy...

Love and warmth are flowing through my feet and legs...

My uterus feels relaxed and full of oxygen rich blood and nutrients....

My ovaries feel relaxed as they prepare for the release

of a unique and remarkable egg(s)...

Warmth and love are flowing from my heart to my uterus and ovaries...

My hands, arms and shoulders feel heavy...

Warmth and heaviness are flowing through my hands and arms...

Warmth and love are flowing through my heart...

My neck, jaw, tongue and forehead feel relaxed and smooth...

My whole body feels quiet, heavy and comfortable...

I am comfortably relaxed...

Warmth and heaviness flow into my arms, hands and fingertips...

My breathing is slow and regular...

I am aware of my calm, regular heartbeat...

I am aware of a deep and abiding love within me...

My mind is becoming quieter as I focus inward...

I feel still...

Deep in my mind I experience myself as relaxed, comfortable and still...

I am alert in a quiet, inward way...

As I color, I take energizing breaths, bringing love and energy into my

heart,

my uterus,

into my ovaries,

and into the egg(s)

that is preparing to be released from my ovary.

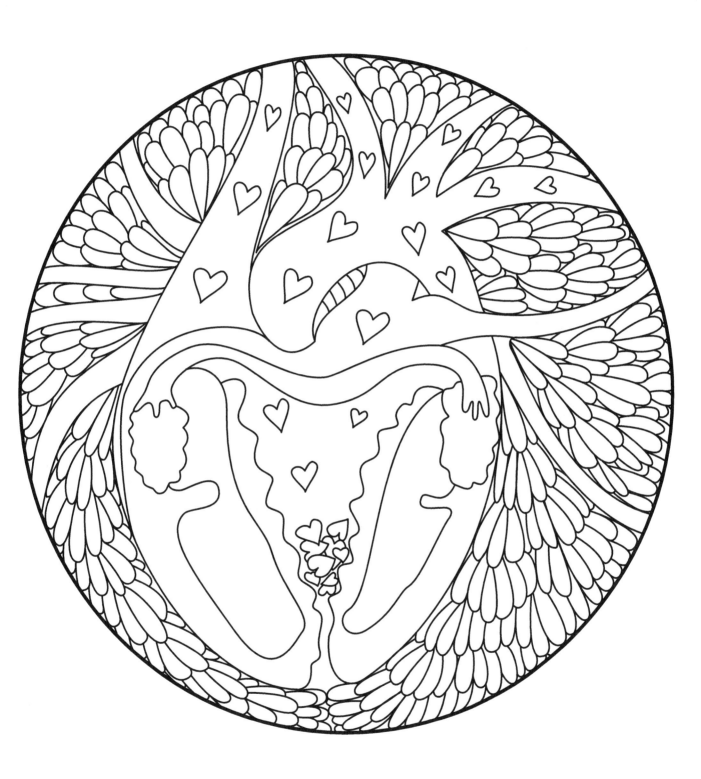

DAY 12

I am beginning to let myself be as I am...

As I accept myself as I am, I let go and more life flows through me...

My feet, knees and hips feel heavy...

Love and warmth are flowing through my feet and legs...

My uterus feels relaxed and full of oxygen rich blood and nutrients....

Warmth and love are flowing from my heart to my uterus and ovaries...

My ovary is releasing a healthy and fully developed egg(s)..

Warmth and love are flowing from my heart to this egg(s)...

My hands, arms and shoulders feel heavy...

Warmth and heaviness are flowing through my hands and arms...

My neck, jaw, tongue and forehead feel relaxed and smooth...

My whole body feels quiet, heavy and comfortable...

I am comfortably relaxed...

Warmth and heaviness flow into my arms, hands and fingertips...

My breathing is slow and regular...

I am aware of my calm, regular heartbeat...

I am aware of a deep and abiding love within me...

I am aware of a surge of lutenizing hormone triggering the release of the egg(s) into my open and clear

fallopian tube...

My mind is becoming quieter as I focus inward...

I feel still...

Deep in my mind I experience myself as relaxed, comfortable and still...

I am alert in a quiet, inward way...

As I color, I take energizing breaths, bringing love and energy into my

heart, my uterus, into my ovaries and into the egg(s)

that is being released from my ovary...

As I color, I bring love and energy into this

healthy and fully developed egg(s).

DAY 13

I am beginning to feel a deep and abiding relaxation within me...

I am beginning to feel full and open...

My feet, knees and hips feel relaxed...

Love and warmth are flowing through my feet and legs...

My uterus feels receptive ....

Cervical mucus is lubricating my cervix...

My ovary is releasing a healthy and fully developed egg(s)...

My hands, arms and shoulders feel heavy...

Warmth and heaviness are flowing through my hands and arms...

Warmth and love are flowing through my heart...

My neck, jaw, tongue and forehead feel relaxed and smooth...

My whole body feels quiet, heavy and comfortable...

I am comfortably relaxed...

Warmth and heaviness flow into my arms, hands and fingertips...

My breathing is slow and regular...

I am aware of my calm, regular heartbeat...

I am aware of a deep and abiding love within me...

I am aware of a surge of lutenizing hormone triggering the release of the egg(s)

into my open and clear fallopian tube...

My mind is becoming quieter as I focus inward...

I feel still...

Deep in my mind I experience myself as relaxed, comfortable and still...

I am alert in a quiet, inward way...

As I color, I take energizing breaths, bringing love and energy into my

cervix,

my uterus,

into my ovaries,

and into the egg(s)

that is being released from my ovary...

As I color, I open to the sperm living

within me protected by my cervical mucus

traveling to fertilize my healthy and fully developed egg(s).

DAY 14

I am beginning to feel a deep and abiding connection within me...

I am beginning to feel secure and at peace...

My feet, knees and hips feel heavy...

Love and warmth are flowing through my feet and legs...

My fallopian tubes feel open and clear...

My ovary is releasing a healthy and fully developed egg(s)

into my fallopian tube...

I feel warmth and relaxation flowing through my reproductive organs...

My hands, arms and shoulders feel heavy...

Warmth and heaviness are flowing through my hands and arms...

My neck, jaw, tongue and forehead feel relaxed and smooth...

My whole body feels quiet, heavy and comfortable...

I am comfortably relaxed...

Warmth and heaviness flow into my arms, hands and fingertips...

My breathing is slow and regular...

I am aware of my calm, regular heartbeat...

I am aware of a deep and abiding love within me...

My mind is becoming quieter as I focus inward...

I feel still...

Deep in my mind I experience myself as relaxed, comfortable and still...

I am alert in a quiet, inward way...

As I color, I take energizing breaths, bringing love and energy into my

fallopian tubes, my uterus, into my ovaries

and into the egg(s)

that is being released from my ovary...

As I color, I bring love and energy into

my heart stimulating its natural tendency to cradle my

fears with its warmth and love.

DAY 15

I continue to feel a deep and abiding connection within me...

I continue to feel secure and at peace...

My feet, knees and hips feel heavy...

Love and warmth are flowing through my feet and legs...

My fallopian tubes feel open and clear...

A very special egg(s) is traveling freely through my open and clear fallopian tube...

I feel warmth and relaxation flowing through my reproductive organs...

My hands, arms and shoulders feel heavy...

Warmth and heaviness are flowing through my hands and arms...

My neck, jaw, tongue and forehead feel relaxed and smooth...

My whole body feels quiet, heavy and comfortable...

I am comfortably relaxed...

Warmth and heaviness flow into my arms, hands and fingertips...

My breathing is slow and regular...

I am aware of my calm, regular heartbeat...

I am aware of a deep and abiding love within me...

My mind is becoming quieter as I focus inward...

I feel still...

Deep in my mind I experience myself as relaxed, comfortable and still...

I am alert in a quiet, inward way...

As I color, I take energizing breaths, bringing love and energy into my

fallopian tubes, my uterus, into my ovaries,

and into the egg(s)

that is being released from my ovary...

As I color, I open to the sperm living within me

protected by my cervical mucus

traveling to fertilize my healthy and fully developed egg(s).

DAY 16

I continue to feel a deep and abiding connection within me...

When I feel connected to myself, I feel relaxed...

My feet, knees and hips feel heavy...

Love and warmth are flowing through my feet and legs...

My fallopian tubes feel open and clear...

The egg(s) that is traveling freely through my open and clear fallopian tube

has completely united with the sperm...

I feel warmth and relaxation flowing through the fertilized egg...

My hands, arms and shoulders feel heavy...

Warmth and heaviness are flowing through my hands and arms...

My neck, jaw, tongue and forehead feel relaxed and smooth...

My whole body feels quiet, heavy and comfortable...

I am comfortably relaxed...

Warmth and heaviness flow into my arms, hands and fingertips...

My breathing is slow and regular...

I am aware of my calm, regular heartbeat...

I am aware of a deep and abiding love within me...

My mind is becoming quieter as I focus inward...

I feel still...

Deep in my mind I experience myself as relaxed, comfortable and still...

I am alert in a quiet, inward way...

As I color, I take energizing breaths, bringing love and energy into my open and clear fallopian tubes

and into the fertilized egg(s) moving toward my uterus...

As I color, I take energizing breaths, bringing love and energy into my awaiting uterus

and into the progesterone helping my uterus prepare

to nurture the fertilized egg(s).

DAY 17

I am beginning to feel more and more at home with myself...

When I come home to myself, I feel relaxed...

My feet, knees and hips feel heavy...

Love and warmth are flowing through my feet and legs...

My fallopian tubes feel open and clear...

The fertilized egg(s) that is traveling freely through my open and clear fallopian tube

is growing and moving toward my uterus...

I feel warmth and relaxation flowing through the fertilized egg...

My hands, arms and shoulders feel heavy...

Warmth and heaviness are flowing through my hands and arms...

My neck, jaw, tongue and forehead feel relaxed and smooth...

My whole body feels quiet, heavy and comfortable...

I am comfortably relaxed...

Warmth and heaviness flow into my arms, hands and fingertips...

My breathing is slow and regular...

I am aware of my calm, regular heartbeat...

I am aware of a deep and abiding love within me...

My mind is becoming quieter as I focus inward...

I feel still...

Deep in my mind I experience myself as relaxed, comfortable and still...

I am alert in a quiet, inward way...

As I color, I take energizing breaths, bringing love and energy into my fallopian tubes

and into the fertilized egg(s) growing and making its way toward my uterus...

As I color, I take energizing breaths, bringing love and energy into my awaiting uterus

and into the progesterone helping my uterus prepare a nest

to nurture and house the fertilized egg(s).

DAY 18

I am beginning to feel more and more familiar with my physiology...

As I become more familiar with myself, I feel increasingly relaxed...

My feet, knees and hips feel heavy...

Love and warmth are flowing through my feet and legs...

My fallopian tubes feel open and clear...

The fertilized egg(s) that is traveling freely through my open and clear fallopian tube

is developing and moving slowly toward my uterus...

I feel warmth and relaxation flowing through the fertilized egg...

My hands, arms and shoulders feel heavy...

Warmth and heaviness are flowing through my hands and arms...

My neck, jaw, tongue and forehead feel relaxed and smooth...

My whole body feels quiet, heavy and comfortable...

I am comfortably relaxed...

Warmth and heaviness flow into my arms, hands and fingertips...

My breathing is slow and regular...

I am aware of my calm, regular heartbeat...

I am aware of a deep and abiding love within me...

My mind is becoming quieter as I focus inward...

I feel still...

Deep in my mind I experience myself as relaxed, comfortable and still...

I am alert in a quiet, inward way...

As I color, I take energizing breaths, bringing love and energy into my fallopian tubes and

into the fertilized egg(s) developing and making its way toward my uterus...

As I color, I take energizing breaths, bringing love and energy into my awaiting uterus

and into the progesterone helping my uterus to prepare a

nutrient rich lining to nurture the fertilized egg(s).

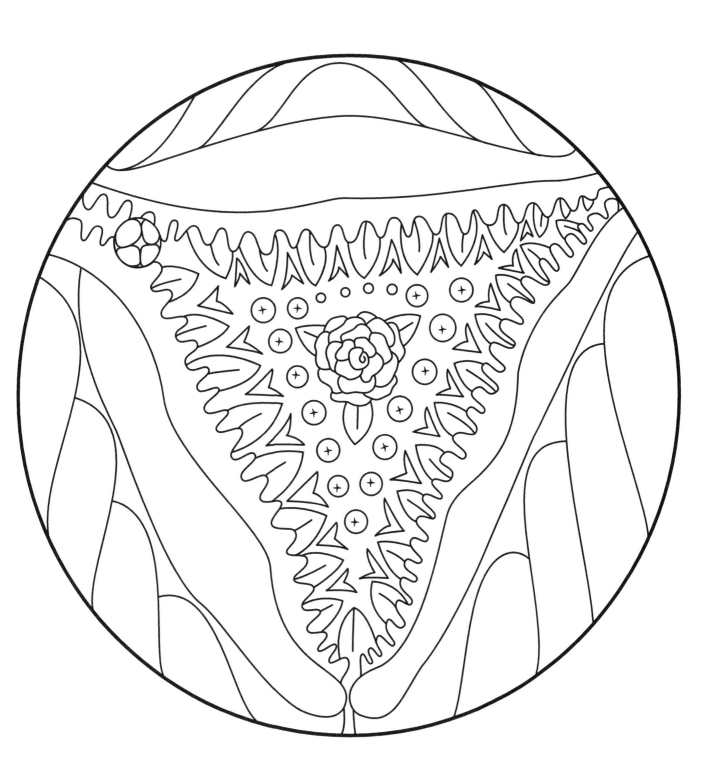

DAY 19

I am beginning to feel more and more comfortable with myself...

As I allow myself to be as I am without any judgment, I feel more and more relaxed...

My feet, knees and hips feel heavy...

Love and warmth are flowing through my feet and legs...

My uterus feels full and welcoming...

The fertilized egg(s) that is traveling freely through my open and clear fallopian tube

is developing slowly and steadily and moving into my uterus...

I feel warmth and relaxation flowing through the fertilized egg

as it moves into my awaiting and receptive uterus...

My hands, arms and shoulders feel heavy...

Warmth and heaviness are flowing through my hands and arms...

My neck, jaw, tongue and forehead feel relaxed and smooth...

My whole body feels quiet, heavy and comfortable...

I am comfortably relaxed...

Warmth and heaviness flow into my arms, hands and fingertips...

My breathing is slow and regular...

I am aware of my calm, regular heartbeat...

I am aware of a deep and abiding love within me...

My mind is becoming quieter as I focus inward...

I feel still...

Deep in my mind I experience myself as relaxed, comfortable and still...

I am alert in a quiet, inward way...

As I color, I take energizing breaths, bringing love and energy into the fertilized egg(s) developing and

making its way into my uterus...

As I color, I take energizing breaths, bringing love and energy into my welcoming uterus

and into the progesterone helping my uterus prepare nutrient rich soil

to nurture and house the fertilized egg(s).

DAY 20

I am beginning to feel the love I have for myself even when fear arises within me...

As I allow myself to feel this love while I feel fear, I feel more and more relaxed...

My feet, knees and hips feel heavy...

Love and warmth are flowing through my feet and legs...

My uterus feels full and welcoming...

I feel warmth and relaxation flowing through the developing blastocyst

as it begins to be received within my uterine wall...

My hands, arms and shoulders feel heavy...

Warmth and heaviness are flowing through my hands and arms...

My neck, jaw, tongue and forehead feel relaxed and smooth...

My whole body feels quiet, heavy and comfortable...

I am comfortably relaxed...

Warmth and heaviness flow into my arms, hands and fingertips...

My breathing is slow and regular...

I am aware of my calm, regular heartbeat...

I am aware of a deep and abiding love within me...

My mind is becoming quieter as I focus inward...

I feel still...

Deep in my mind I experience myself as relaxed, comfortable and still...

I am alert in a quiet, inward way...

As I color, I take energizing breaths, bringing love and energy into my nourished uterus...

As I color, I take energizing breaths, bringing love and energy into the blastocyst, as it hatches from

the zona pellucida and begins to embed into the lining of my uterus.

DAY 21

I am beginning to feel the deep love I have for myself ...

As I allow myself to feel this abiding love, I feel more and more balanced...

My feet, knees and hips feel heavy...

Love and warmth are flowing through my feet and legs...

My uterus feels nutrient rich, full and welcoming...

I feel warmth and relaxation flowing through my blossoming uterus...

My hands, arms and shoulders feel heavy...

Warmth and heaviness are flowing through my hands and arms...

My neck, jaw, tongue and forehead feel relaxed and smooth...

My whole body feels quiet, heavy and comfortable...

I am comfortably relaxed...

Warmth and heaviness flow into my arms, hands and fingertips...

My breathing is slow and regular...

I am aware of my calm, regular heartbeat...

I am aware of a deep and abiding love within me...

My mind is becoming quieter as I focus inward...

I feel still...

Deep in my mind I experience myself as relaxed, comfortable and still...

I am alert in a quiet, inward way...

As I color, I take energizing breaths, bringing love and energy into the blastocyst embedding

further into the lining of my uterus...

As I color, I take energizing breaths, bringing love and energy into every cell in my body.

DAY 22

I am beginning to feel deeply nourished...

As I nourish myself, my body is able to do more and more nourishing...

My feet, knees and hips feel heavy...

Love and warmth are flowing through my feet and legs...

My uterus feels full and welcoming...

My hormones are balanced...

I feel warmth and relaxation flowing through my uterus

and the blastocyst growing within my uterine wall...

My hands, arms and shoulders feel heavy...

Warmth and heaviness are flowing through my hands and arms...

My neck, jaw, tongue and forehead feel relaxed and smooth...

My whole body feels quiet, heavy and comfortable...

I am comfortably relaxed...

Warmth and heaviness flow into my arms, hands and fingertips...

My breathing is slow and regular...

I am aware of my calm, regular heartbeat...

I am aware of a deep and abiding love within me...

My mind is becoming quieter as I focus inward...

I feel still...

Deep in my mind I experience myself as relaxed, comfortable and still...

I am alert in a quiet, inward way...

As I color, I take energizing breaths, bringing love and energy into my uterus...

As I color, I take energizing breaths, bringing love and energy into my endocrine system

which is helping my uterus to nurture and grow the implanted blastocyst.

DAY 23

I am continuing to feel deeply nourished...

As I nourish myself, my body is able to do more and more nourishing...

My feet, knees and hips feel heavy...

Love and warmth are flowing through my feet and legs...

My uterus feels full and nutrient rich...

My hormones are balanced...

I feel warmth and relaxation flowing through my uterus...

The blastocyst is becoming securely implanted in my uterine lining...

My hands, arms and shoulders feel heavy...

Warmth and heaviness are flowing through my hands and arms...

My neck, jaw, tongue and forehead feel relaxed and smooth...

My whole body feels quiet, heavy and comfortable...

I am comfortably relaxed...

Warmth and heaviness flow into my arms, hands and fingertips...

My breathing is slow and regular...

I am aware of my calm, regular heartbeat...

I am aware of a deep and abiding love within me...

My mind is becoming quieter as I focus inward...

I feel still...

Deep in my mind I experience myself as relaxed, comfortable and still...

I am alert in a quiet, inward way...

As I color, I take energizing breaths, bringing love and energy into the hormones circulating

in my bloodstream,

nurturing the developing blastocyst securely attached to my endometrium.

DAY 24

I am beginning to soften and open...

As I soften and open to life, life more freely moves through me...

My feet, knees and hips feel heavy...

Love and warmth are flowing through my feet and legs...

My uterus feels full and overflowing...

I feel light and energy flowing through my uterus...

My hands, arms and shoulders feel heavy...

Warmth and heaviness are flowing through my hands and arms...

My neck, jaw, tongue and forehead feel relaxed and smooth...

My whole body feels quiet, heavy and comfortable...

I am comfortably relaxed...

Warmth and heaviness flow into my arms, hands and fingertips...

My breathing is slow and regular...

I am aware of my calm, regular heartbeat...

I am aware of a deep and abiding love within me...

My mind is becoming quieter as I focus inward...

I feel still...

Deep in my mind I experience myself as relaxed, comfortable and still...

I am alert in a quiet, inward way...

As I color, I take energizing breaths, bringing love and energy into my uterus
and into my heart...

As I color, I take energizing breaths, bringing love and energy into the
blastocyst securely implanted in my endometrium...

As I color, I take energizing breaths, bringing love and energy
into every cell in my body.

DAY 25

I am beginning to feel incredibly vital...

As my vitality blossoms, my body surrenders...

My feet, knees and hips feel heavy...

Love and warmth are flowing through my feet and legs...

My uterus feels full of energy...

I feel warmth and relaxation flowing through my uterus...

My hands, arms and shoulders feel heavy...

Warmth and heaviness are flowing through my hands and arms...

My neck, jaw, tongue and forehead feel relaxed and smooth...

My whole body feels quiet, heavy and comfortable...

I am comfortably relaxed...

Warmth and heaviness flow into my arms, hands and fingertips...

My breathing is slow and regular...

I am aware of my calm, regular heartbeat...

I am aware of a deep and abiding love within me...

My mind is becoming quieter as I focus inward...

I feel still...

Deep in my mind I experience myself as relaxed, comfortable and still...

I am alert in a quiet, inward way...

As I color, I take energizing breaths, bringing love and energy into my uterus

and the forming placenta.

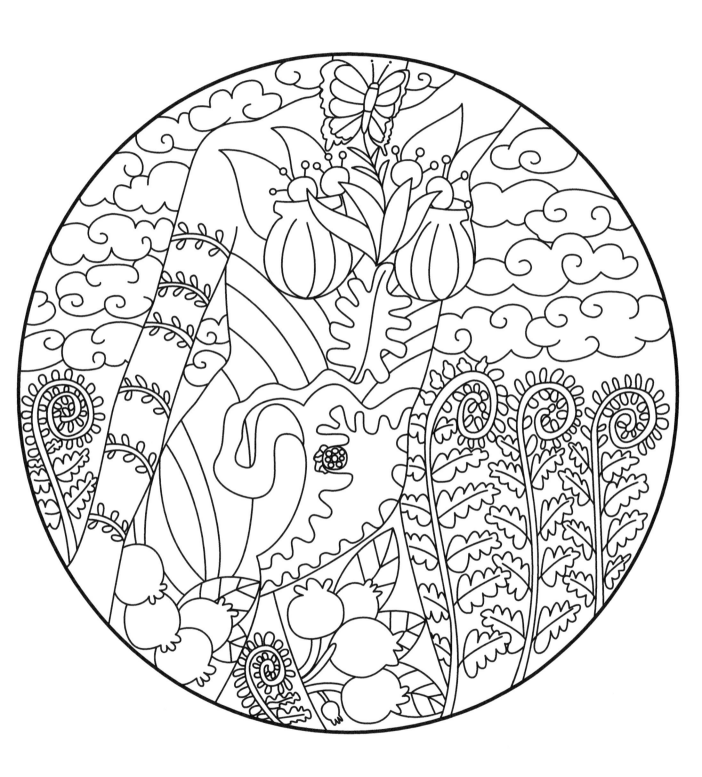

DAY 26

I continue to feel incredibly vital...

As my vitality blossoms, my body regulates...

My feet, knees and hips feel heavy...

Love and warmth are flowing through my feet and legs...

My uterus feels full of life...

The placenta is growing and nurturing the developing embryo...

My hands, arms and shoulders feel heavy...

Warmth and heaviness are flowing through my hands and arms...

My neck, jaw, tongue and forehead feel relaxed and smooth...

My whole body feels quiet, heavy and comfortable...

I am comfortably relaxed...

Warmth and heaviness flow into my arms, hands and fingertips...

My breathing is slow and regular...

I am aware of my calm, regular heartbeat...

I am aware of a deep and abiding love within me...

My mind is becoming quieter as I focus inward...

I feel still...

Deep in my mind I experience myself as relaxed, comfortable and still...

I am alert in a quiet, inward way...

As I color, I take energizing breaths, bringing love and energy into my uterus
and into every cell in my body...

As I color, I take energizing breaths, bringing love and energy into my endocrine
system, which is helping my placenta to form
to nurture and grow the securely implanted embryo.

DAY 27

I continue to feel relaxed and secure...

As I relax, my body is able to do more and more nurturing...

My feet, knees and hips feel heavy...

Love and warmth are flowing through my feet and legs...

My uterus feels full, thick and round...

The embryo is developing within the loving embrace of my uterus...

My hands, arms and shoulders feel heavy...

Warmth and heaviness are flowing through my hands and arms...

My neck, jaw, tongue and forehead feel relaxed and smooth...

My whole body feels quiet, heavy and comfortable...

I am comfortably relaxed...

Warmth and heaviness flow into my arms, hands and fingertips...

My breathing is slow and regular...

I am aware of my calm, regular heartbeat...

I am aware of a deep and abiding love within me...

My mind is becoming quieter as I focus inward...

I feel still...

Deep in my mind I experience myself as relaxed, comfortable and still...

I am alert in a quiet, inward way...

As I color, I take energizing breaths, bringing love and energy into my uterus

and into every cell in my body.

DAY 28

I am beginning to feel incredibly peaceful and calm...

When I feel at peace with things as they are,

my body and mind are able to experience the uncertainties of life ...

My feet, knees and hips feel heavy...

Love and warmth are flowing through my feet and legs...

My uterus feels full and welcoming...

My hormones are regulated...

I feel warmth and relaxation flowing through my reproductive organs...

My hands, arms and shoulders feel heavy...

Warmth and heaviness are flowing through my hands and arms...

My neck, jaw, tongue and forehead feel relaxed and smooth...

My whole body feels quiet, heavy and comfortable...

I am comfortably relaxed...

Warmth and heaviness flow into my arms, hands and fingertips...

My breathing is slow and regular...

I am aware of my calm, regular heartbeat...

I am aware of a deep and abiding love within me...

My mind is becoming quieter as I focus inward...

I feel still...

Deep in my mind I experience myself as relaxed, comfortable and still...

I am alert in a quiet, inward way...

As I color, I take energizing breaths, bringing love and energy into my uterus

and into every cell in my body...

As I color, I take energizing breaths, bringing love and energy into all possible realities,

all possible outcomes,

without blame and without judgment,

welcoming all of life within me.

Buffy Trupp, MA, RCC, LMFT, is a somatic psychotherapist and founder of the Mindful Fertility Project. She has been teaching mindfulness to women and couples trying to conceive since 2006 with astonishing results. She is the author of the clinically proven *Mindful Fertility Journal:* a comprehensive, virtual, research–proven mindfulness–based program for fertility. Her website is www.mindfulfertilityproject.com

Arla Patch, BFA, Ed., MFA, is a teaching artist who uses art as a tool for healing. Her own trauma history was the motivation for healing and as an artist she turned to creativity. Once she discovered the transformative power of art-making she began sharing it with others in classes and workshops. She has worked with incarcerated women and incarcerated youth, at-risk teens, women who have survived breast cancer, domestic violence and sexual abuse. Arla's interest in healing also led to her involvement with the first truth commission in the United States, the Maine Wabanaki-State Child Welfare Truth and Reconciliation Commission. This commission was formed to look into what happened to native children in Maine in the child welfare system. Arla is the award-winning author of two books: *A Body Story,* and *Finding Ground: Girls and Women in Recovery.* Her website is www.arlapatch.com.

CPSIA information can be obtained
at www.ICGtesting.com
Printed in the USA
LVOW06s1726211117
556996LV00005BB/50/P